The Odyssey of John Chillag, a Hungarian Jew Born in Vienna

From Györ in Hungary to Australia and England

via Auschwitz and Buchenwald

The Odyssey of John Chillag, a Hungarian Jew Born in Vienna

From Györ in Hungary to Australia and England via Auschwitz and Buchenwald

John Chillag
interviewed in
Bochum, Germany,
by Hubert Schneider

THE
HOLOCAUST
CENTRE

BETH SHALOM

The Odyssey of John Chillag, a Hungarian Jew Born in Vienna

From Györ in Hungary to Australia and England
via Auschwitz and Buchenwald

John Chillag interviewed in Bochum, Germany, by Hubert Schneider

Based on – but substantially enhanced in text and illustrations –
Chapter 5 of the book in German, first published in 2002 in Germany
by Verlag und Druckkontor Kamp GmbH, Bochum under the title:
*...und die Erinnerung tragen wir im Herzen – Briefe ehemaliger
Zwangsarbeiter – Bochum 1942-1945*
Edited by Waltraud Jachnow, Sabine Kraemer, Wilfried Korngiebel,
Susanne Slobodzian for and on behalf of the initiative "Entschädigung
jetzt".
©The Editors and Individual Contributors, 2002
©Verlag und Druckkontor Kamp GmbH, Bochum, 2002

This partial – but in parts enhanced – English version (mainly of
Chapter 5, pp. 204-227) is first published in the UK in 2004 by The
Holocaust Centre, Beth Shalom, under the title:
The Odyssey of John Chillag, a Hungarian Jew Born in Vienna.
*From Györ in Hungary to Australia and England via Auschwitz and
Buchenwald.*

English version ©The Holocaust Centre and J. P. Chillag, 2004
Second Edition, April 2006
ISBN 0-9543001-2-2
    978-0-9543001-2-8

Dedicated to my wife,
children and grandchildren;
and in memory of my parents
and the 60 members
of my extended family
who perished in Auschwitz,
Bochum and other camps,
in labour battalions
and on death marches

"That the generations to come might know..."
(Psalms, 78:6)

Foreword

The unique slave labour graves in the Jewish cemetery on the Wasserstrasse, Bochum

In the final months of Nazi Germany, Bochum was the 'home' of a large number of slave labour camps. These included an external camp of Buchenwald: the *Bochumer Verein KZ* on the Brüllstrasse, adjacent to the largest armament works in the Third Reich. The slave labourers in this camp included John Csillag and his father József. John's father succumbed to the atrocious conditions at the heavy steel presses and died in the camp on 5 December 1944. The normal method of disposing of the prisoners' corpses was cremation, with the ashes scattered to the winds.

John, the only survivor of a large family of 60, enquired in the early 1950s through the *Red Cross International Tracing Service* whether there was any information on the fate of any of his family members. The Red Cross could only trace two people – John and his father; all the others had perished in the gas chambers of Auschwitz-Birkenau. The certificate on John's father ended with the words "and he is buried in Bochum Wiemelhausen Jewish cemetery." It was a most improbable story, but it was true, and unravelling the full facts took over half a century.

A few days before the death of József Csillag, the RAF flattened the city, its factories and crematoria in three successive heavy air raids. With the crematoria out of action, the Camp's SS commandant did not know what to do with corpses and sent a teletype message to his superiors in Buchenwald for 'orders'. The terse response was, "Bury them." The first name listed on the teletype (slightly misspellt) was that of John's father. So his remains – and later those of 51 other victims – were dumped at Bochum's Jewish cemetery, where one might have expected them to rest in unmarked mass graves. Yet when John had his first chance to visit the cemetery in 1963, he found a setting rather like a 'war cemetery': two rows of 52 well-maintained individual graves, all with identical grave stones, each with the name and details of the body buried beneath. One of these graves is the resting place of József Csillag.

How did all this happen? To get to the beginning of the story, one has to turn back the pages of history to 1933. Steel and coal were the mainstay of Bochum and all the Ruhr region, and many workers in these industries were – to put it mildly – politically 'left-of-centre'. As soon as Hitler came to power, Bernhard Haltern, then a young socialist activist steel-worker, joined the Nazi party. This was not for ideological reasons, but purely to cover the tracks of his political activities, which he continued, although probably more cautiously. In due course, he was rewarded by the Nazis with his appointment as superintendent of Bochum Wiemelhausen cemetery. In the aftermath of *Kristallnacht* and later, Haltern used his position to protect the Jewish section of the cemetery from vandalism by Nazi thugs. After November 1944, when bodies of Jewish slave labourers were dumped in the cemetery, he and his wife jotted down details (usually the *Häftlingnummer*, the prisoner number), then arranged for the victims to be buried – not in mass graves, but in individual graves, each marked with the victim's identity.

In the early 1960s Bochum's municipal authority arranged for rows of headstones to be erected over the graves, each engraved with the victim's name and details, in the style of a 'war cemetery'.

Today, these well-kept graves are 'protected monuments' in a situation unique in the annals of the Holocaust.

The Odyssey of John Chillag, a Hungarian Jew Born in Vienna

From Győr in Hungary to Australia and England via Auschwitz and Buchenwald

John Chillag[1] interviewed in Bochum, Germany, by Hubert Schneider

Introduction

Entering the Jewish cemetery[2] on the Wasserstrasse in Bochum, the visitor's first impression is of the large number of well-maintained, imposing monumental stones. However, one also observes that in the back rows of Field V, the gravestones become gradually smaller and plainer, until by the beginning of Row 4, the cover stones have become anything but elaborate. Further along this row, there are many gaps until one reaches a sequence of uniform, identical headstones, a line extending to the back row and also continuing into the middle of the first row of Field W. An explanation can be found in the Jewish history of Bochum in the decade between 1935 and 1945. As a result of public

1

persecution, the increasing deprivation of rights, loss of economic livelihoods and the so-called 'Aryanization', Jews no longer found it possible to erect 'decent' gravestones. Indeed, they were often unable to afford any stones at all.

What one sees next, in rows V.F. 26 to W.A. 13, are 52 gravestones in light-coloured Ruhr sandstone, all of identical appearance. The names on the stones sound foreign and strange to German ears. The graves contain the remains of men only, all of whom died between 5 December 1944 and 16 March 1945. A little research reveals that the men buried here were all slave labour victims of the *SS-Aussenkommando Bochumer Verein*, a work *Kommando* (work unit) under the external control of KZ (*Konzentrationslager*: concentration camp) Buchenwald. At a time when Germany was already *Judenrein* and 'cleansed' of its indigenous Jews, these were Hungarian Jews, taken as slave labourers to Bochum in the second half of 1944. They were either taken directly from Auschwitz and later transferred to KZ Buchenwald, or transported via Buchenwald to Bochum. The normal procedure for the disposal of dead Jewish slave labourers was cremation, often without leaving any trace, but occasionally with a prisoner number recorded. This group of prisoners was only buried because the crematoria in Bochum and Essen had been demolished by Allied bombing raids.

In 1965 the municipality of Bochum erected uniform headstones over the graves in the cemetery and has maintained the plots ever since. The graveyard itself has been designated a 'protected monument'. In between the 52 uniform graves, there is just one that looks different. A surviving son of Lipót Weiss who was buried there did not accept the municipality's offer and erected a personal gravestone with an inscription commemorating not just his father, but also his mother and their four children who were murdered in Auschwitz.

How did Hungarian Jews come to be in Bochum, Germany, in the second half of 1944? Their presence raises a few questions. In a 1993 publication of the *Vereinigung der Verfolgten des Naziregimes – Bund der Antifaschisten (VVN)*[3] one reads:

"From July 1943 the *Bochumer Verein* also used concentration camp prisoners as slave labourers. Initially, these prisoners were dispersed into a number of heavily guarded *Ostarbeiter* [forced labour] camps. At the beginning of 1944, the [Third] Reich's Ministry for Armament and War Production [led by Albert Speer], the *Waffen-SS* and the board of the *Bochumer Verein* jointly agreed to increase the use of concentration camp prisoners and to establish a KZ Branch Camp within the *Bochumer Verein* (in its ammunition works). The preparatory work necessary for this included sending teams of *Bochumer Verein* directors and managers to KZ branch camps which were already operational to study the security arrangements, and to the concentration camps in Auschwitz and Buchenwald to 'select' a slave labour work force. Not much later, an SS team arrived in Bochum to inspect the existing work camp in the Brüllstrasse. Soon after that, an advance SS unit arrived to supervise the building arrangements for the new camp, together with some concentration camp prisoners who were set to work on the construction of further barracks, the high-voltage electrified fences and the network of roads, etc. On 26 July 1944, with the arrival of 434 Hungarian Jews transferred from Auschwitz via Buchenwald, the camp on the Brüllstrasse became 'operational'. This was followed in August by a further shipment of Jews from various European countries. The entry in the *Auschwitz Chronicle 1939-1945*[4] for 20 August 1944 includes the following: '270 prisoners – Hungarian Jews – are transferred from KL Auschwitz to KL Buchenwald, to its 'Auxiliary Camp' Bochum.' A further 500 Jews reached the Camp in Bochum from KZ Neuengamme. The number of these slave labourers in the armament works rapidly rose to 1,213, and by November 1944 it had reached 1,706. These concentration camp prisoners were almost exclusively Jews, and were brutally treated by their SS guards."

As the theatre of war came ever closer to Bochum and Wattenscheid, on 21 March 1945 1,361 prisoners were evacuated from the Branch Camp in the Brüllstrasse and transported by rail to KZ Buchenwald. The train reached Buchenwald with 1,326 prisoners on March 23. Nothing further is known about the fate of these prisoners .....[5]

As the booklet states, "Nothing further is known about the fate of these prisoners...." And nothing is known about the future faced by these prisoners, nor their earlier life. They only surface as a collective group without any individuality. For example, the *Auschwitz Chronicle* records the arrival of the first Jews on 14 June 1944 as follows:

> Six female Jews, twin sisters, receive Nos. A-7216–A-7221 after selection from an RSHA (*Reichssicherheitshauptamt*: Reich Security Main Office) transport from Hungary and are admitted to the camp. Some of the people in this transport are probably killed; the young and healthy are kept in the camp as 'depot prisoners' (transit prisoners).[6]

The twins were taken into the camp for research purposes; those deemed suitable for work were not given prisoner numbers, but were earmarked as 'depot prisoners' or slave labour for the German armament industry, and those unsuitable for work were murdered. But there was no information at all about who these people were. And in the entry for 20 August (as we have already seen from the VVN booklet), the *Chronicle* states, "270 prisoners – Hungarian Jews – are transferred from KL Auschwitz to KL Buchenwald, to the 'Auxiliary' Camp of Bochum."[7] These 270 men were taken directly from Auschwitz to Bochum and only later transferred to Buchenwald's 'books'.[8] And we still knew nothing about the individuals concerned.

When the VVN booklet was published in 1995, its authors had no knowledge whatsoever of these Hungarian Jewish men who were 'imported' as slave labourers into Bochum. It is thanks to John Chillag, who now lives in Great Britain, that today we know quite a lot more about them. On 5 February 1999 John wrote a letter to Hans Frankenthal of the *Jüdisches Landesverband* in Dortmund,[9] which reads (in part):

> I am a Holocaust survivor who – at the age of 17 – was transported in August 1944 with 270 other Hungarian Jews from Auschwitz to Bochum, where we worked as slave labourers at the then *Bochumer Verein Gussstahl* works. Incidentally, my father died in the camp in Bochum and is buried with others who died there in Wiemelhausen Jewish cemetery. Whenever I am not too far from Bochum (about every couple of years), I visit the cemetery there. It is possible that I will be travelling through Bochum again this April.
>
> I wonder whether you and/or the *Landesverband* have any documentation or details about this particular Buchenwald *Aussenkommando*, the BVG (*Bochumer Verein für Gußstahlfabrikation*) buildings in question, or any other details. I know that the *Stadtgemeinde* (municipality) in Essen produced a book on some of the camps in their area. Did Bochum perhaps do something similar, or would the *Stadt-Archiv* in Bochum have some information?
>
> I was evacuated to Buchenwald in March 1945, went back to Hungary later that year, and then to Australia in 1950. I spent the first part of my working life there, but have lived in England since 1963. Since my retirement I regularly give talks on my Holocaust experiences to students and other groups in schools and universities... "[10]

Hans Frankenthal (who sadly has now passed away) was not too familiar with the situation in Bochum and passed the letter on to the *Erinnern für die Zukunft* (Remembering for the Future) association in Bochum, asking them to reply directly to Mr Chillag. Some relevant brochures were enclosed with the reply, including the 1995 VVN publication mentioned above. Mr Chillag replied by return post:

> This is my story; I was one of the 270 people who arrived in Bochum from Auschwitz on 21 August 1944. The transport also included my father, who lost his life in Bochum and is buried in the cemetery there. I was one of those people, at that stage more dead than alive, who were evacuated in March 1945 from Bochum to Buchenwald. I can tell you a lot about the fate of the 270 men. And I will be in Bochum shortly!

An intensive exchange of letters followed, and since then John Chillag has been to Bochum a number of times. We found out not only about his own story and the fate of his family in the Holocaust, but he also had a wealth of information about the others who lie in the graves in Wiemelhausen.

So now when we walk along the row of graves on the Wasserstrasse, we see not only rows of uniform, identical gravestones with foreign-sounding names inscribed on them, but we can put a face and a history to those names.

John Chillag recounted his own story and that of his family in an interview with the author, Hubert Schneider, on 9 June 1999. The transcript of that interview, checked, amended and translated by John Chillag, is printed below. In order to understand some details better, it is important to begin with a brief history of Hungarian Jewry, before and after the German occupation of Hungary.[11]

The population census of 1941 numbered Hungary's Jewish population at 725,007. The settlement of Jews in the Hungary of today dates back to Roman times. In more recent times, Hungarian Jewish communities became fully assimilated into the economic and cultural life of the country. Between the second half of the nineteenth century and the first World War, in a country populated by a large number of minority groups, the Jews supported the Magyars in their fight for autonomy. Thus, most Hungarian Jews considered themselves first and foremost Hungarians! This identification with Hungarian nationalism remained in spite of increasing antisemitism in the years between the two world wars. It also defined the reactions of Hungarian Jews during the Second World War.

Following the short-lived dictatorship of the proletariat of Béla Kun in 1919, the non-Jewish majority of the population pushed the 'Jewish Question' to the fore, and it gained further ground during the 1930s. Demands for the 'solution' to this question were voiced by various pro-national socialist parties and movements, and by the Christian churches. The anti-Jewish climate was encouraged by the mass media, mainly the predominantly German-financed press. The Hungarian army was one of the most radical and aggressively antisemitic forces in Hungary. A Hungarian law of May 1938 limited the percentage of Jews in the liberal professions and commerce to 20%, and in May 1939 the permitted percentage of Jews in commerce was reduced to 6%. As a result, discrimination against Jews increased considerably, culminating in the 'Race Laws' of 1941, which were similar to the 1935 Nuremberg Laws in Germany.

In 1940, under the command of the Hungarian army, Hungary also introduced 'Labour Service' for Jewish men of military age. Jews in the Labour Service could not bear arms or wear a military uniform. They were organised into battalions and companies, and had to perform duties on 'important defence projects', including road construction and repair, tree-felling in forests, digging trenches and building anti-tank defences in the country, as well as service on the front in the Ukraine and Serbia, where one of their principal tasks was mine-clearing. Almost 42,000 Hungarian Jews lost their lives in these labour-battalions, which highlights the harsh conditions they had to endure.[12]

Long before the German occupation of the country on 19 March 1944, other Jews who were not in the labour battalions were murdered by Hungarians, often in collaboration with their German 'ideological friends'. In July and August 1941, for example, 17,000 'alien' Jews (those without Hungarian citizenship) were arrested and deported to a place near Kamenez-Podolsk (now called Kamenets Podolsky). There they were murdered along with local, indigenous Galician Jews, by SS and German field police units commanded by *SS-Obergruppenführer* Friedrich Jekeln.

Apart from this atrocity, Hungarian Jews felt relatively safe for the time being, even though they were suffering under considerable restrictions of their civic rights and economic opportunities. Time and again, Miklós Kállay's government (March 1942–March 1944) rejected German demands that Hungary, like other German-dominated countries of Europe, should adopt a programme for a Final Solution for its Jews. This action contributed to the Hungarian Jewish leaders' belief in the conservative-aristocratic regime; they were convinced that Hungary, as a member of the Axis-Pact, would retain its sovereignty.

These illusions were shattered when German forces occupied Hungary on 19 March 1944. The Germans knew that the Kállay government was negotiating to withdraw from the war with the help of the Western allies. Kállay was immediately replaced by the pro-Nazi leader Döme Sztójay. The occupation forces included an *Einsatzkommando* (special task group set up to 'liquidate' Jews, Gypsies, Communists) led by Adolf Eichmann, whose main task was the provision of technical support and back-up for the rapid execution of the 'Final Solution' in Hungary. The regime initiated many anti-Jewish decrees and provided a special unit with state powers to assist in getting rid of the Jews from the country.

On 15 April 1944, leading Hungarian antisemites, led by Zoltán Bosnyák, established the 'Hungarian Institute for Research into the Jewish Question'. The Institute was advised and 'supervised' by *SS-Hauptsturmbannführer* Heinz Ballensiefen, an 'expert' in anti-Jewish propaganda, and was a virtual replica of its German counterpart, the 'Institute for Research into the Jewish Question' in Berlin.

The Institute's statutes defined its main aim as "to research the Jewish Question in Hungary in a systematic and scientific manner, collect and evaluate data on this subject, making the Hungarian public fully aware of Hungarian and Jewish questions". The Institute published a newspaper entitled *Harc* (Combat), very much along the lines of Julius Streicher's *Der Stürmer*.

Anti-Jewish decrees enforced the isolation, identification, expropriation, ghettoization, concentration and deportation of the Jews. Travel restrictions were imposed, telephones disconnected, radios confiscated, and from 5 April 1944, wearing of a 'yellow star' became compulsory. These measures were followed by the confiscation and expropriation of Jewish businesses, industrial concerns and financial institutions, as well as the closure of law and medical practices. Personal property of Jews was also confiscated, including valuables, bank accounts and jewellery. Although the decree for ghettoization was not published until 28 April 1944, Jews in Trans-Carpathia and Northern Hungary had already been moved into ghettos on 16 April, the first day of the Jewish Passover. At dawn, they were ordered to pack and leave their homes within half an hour. Most of these homes were then ransacked.

In country areas, Jews were first gathered together in local synagogues or community centres, then a few days later they were transferred to ghettos in major country towns. In some cities, the ghettos were established in the main Jewish quarter; elsewhere they were located in brickworks or derelict factory buildings, and sometimes the Jews were forced to camp under open skies. The ghettos were completely sealed off and guarded by local police and gendarmes from other parts of the country. Internally, every ghetto was run by a Jewish Council or *Judenrat*, usually consisting of prominent members of the former Jewish community. The Jewish Council had a line of communication with the Central Jewish Council in Budapest. However, the ghettos existed only for short periods of one to six weeks. The Jews suffered in the bad conditions, with the lack of food and poor sanitation facilities, while the more prosperous Jews in the ghetto were brutally mistreated by the police and gendarmes, to force them to disclose under torture details of any 'hidden assets'.[13]

The deportation of the Jews followed a predetermined geographical pattern. In the rapidly worsening military situation for the Axis-countries, as Soviet forces were crossing Rumania's borders, Eichmann's *Einsatzkommandos* concentrated their efforts on the rapid annihilation of the mainly Orthodox and Chassidic Jewish communities of Trans-Carpathia, followed by those in the northern, southern and western parts of Hungary.

According to Hungarian sources, 434,351 Jews were deported mainly from country regions to Auschwitz.[14] Between 15 May and 9 July 1944, these unfortunates were despatched from 55 main ghettos and centres in 147 hermetically-sealed goods trains. On arrival in Auschwitz, the men, women and children deemed unfit for work were marched straight to the gas chambers. Those selected as fit for work, called *Depotjuden* in SS jargon, were earmarked to be taken as slave labour for German industry in the next weeks. When the Hungarian Regent, Miklós Horthy, stopped the deportations on 7 July 1944, with the exception of Budapest, the whole of the country was already *Judenfrei* (cleansed of its Jews). A few transports with about 21,000 Jews from southern Hungary were sent to Strasshof[15] near Vienna to await the result of negotiations between Zionists and the SS.[16] Most of these Jews survived.

From June 1944, Budapest's Jews were forced to live in designated houses marked with a 'yellow star', but although at times danger threatened, this relatively safe period continued until it came to an abrupt end on 15 October 1944. On the day after Horthy's unsuccessful attempt to withdraw Hungary from the war (he had to cancel an armistice he had just signed with the Soviet Union), the National Socialist Arrow Cross Party took power with the help of the Germans. Thousands of Jews – mainly women – were taken in forced marches to the border of Germany, to build entrenchments for the defence of Vienna. In Budapest, armed Arrow Cross thugs roamed the city, attacking and killing Jews. Many victims were shot on the banks of the Danube. During the Soviet siege of Budapest at the beginning of December 1944, 70,000 Jews were confined to a ghetto in the Jewish quarter of town. Although the ghetto only existed for a short period – it was liberated on 17-18 January 1945 – thousands died there of illness, hunger and cold.

During the war, the Hungarian Jewish community lost 564,500 people, 63,000 of them before the German occupation.

Dr Hubert Schneider, born 1941. Historian at the Ruhr-University Bochum (RUB) and chairman of "Remembering for the Future" Association, Bochum. His recent publications are on the history of the Bochum Jewish community.

The Interview

Hubert Schneider (HS): Mr Chillag, tell me something about your family.

John Chillag (JC): During the First World War, my father was in the army, serving in the Transport Corps. At the end of the War, when there was a revolution in Hungary (as happened in many European countries), he was appointed Movement Officer in the town of Györ, a major railhead. When the revolution collapsed a few months later, he thought it prudent to emigrate and he found asylum first in Germany, and then in Austria – in Vienna. That was in 1920, when he was 24 years old. In Vienna he met my mother. They got married in 1921 and I was born in 1927. At that time, political life in Austria was probably more turbulent than in Germany. There were frequent shootings and streetfights in Vienna and after a while my father thought it might be safer to return to Hungary. So the family moved back in 1934. The Csillag family had a building materials business in Györ, and on our return there, my father joined the firm as their accountant. My grandmother had founded the firm after the death of her husband (my grandfather) in 1911, because she wanted to provide security for herself and her then young children. Her oldest child worked in the firm, and my grandmother never missed a day's work until her death at the age of 85, shortly before the German occupation of Hungary – on 29 December 1943, I think. Technically Hungary was at war, but in practice it was only on the Russian front. In March 1944 all this changed overnight. What took the Nazis years to achieve in Germany, and was done in a shorter and shorter time in the successive countries they overran, took only a couple of weeks in Hungary. I am referring of course to their treatment of Jews.

HS: How large was the Jewish community in Györ?

JC: The Jewish community consisted of about 5,000 people. The total population of the town was about 50,000, so it was a large community. The proportion of Jews was even larger in my mother's hometown, just a few miles away on the other side of the Danube. There the total population was 10,000, and 6,000 of them Jews. It was the town with the highest percentage of Jewish population in the whole of Hungary and Slovakia. In that town, Dunajska Streda/ Dunaszerdahely, Jews were very Orthodox, although my mother was agnostic.

HS: And what sort of community was it in Györ?

JC: Most members of the Jewish community there were very assimilated Jews. Only a small number – perhaps 10 per cent – were Orthodox.

HS: What was Jewish life like in Györ? What sort of organisations existed?

JC: There was a Jewish primary school – that was the school Jewish children went to first. Then at the age of ten or eleven, you went to a public school. I attended a *Gymnasium* (grammar school), the 'Révai Miklós Gimnázium'. There were about 36-37 boys in the class, and five of us were Jews. There was also another boys grammar school in town, with 2-3 Jews in my age group. The situation was very similar in the two girls' grammar schools in town, with eight Jewish girls of my age. There were a number of Jewish welfare and social organisations in town – I think that is so wherever Jews live. There were also many older Jewish men who had fought in the 1914-18 war, some of them highly decorated. In the main synagogue, there was a memorial inscribed with the names of some 150 Jewish men who had fallen in the war, including some members of my family. There was also a book about the history of the Jews of Györ from the Middle Ages to the twentieth century (see Note 17). It was published in Györ in 1930, in Hungarian of course. The book was written by one of my uncles, the husband of one of my father's sisters, who was employed in the town's tax office. And it shows how liberal the Hungarian authorities were at that time because in 1940 he was appointed director of the tax office! This uncle was more religious than you would expect. He was not Orthodox, but he was certainly the most religious member of the family – although that's not saying a lot! Nevertheless, he wrote this book about the Jews of the town.[17] My family had been living in Györ since at least the eighteenth century. In 1979, a second volume on the Jews of Györ was published, covering the period 1930-1947.[18]

HS: What happened to this uncle who wrote the book about the Jews of Györ? Did he survive?

JC: No, unfortunately not; he perished in Auschwitz. Only about 400 of the original 5,000 members of the Jewish community survived. Some were survivors of the camps, but the majority were men from the Labour Battalions.

HS: Slave labourers?

JC: No, these men were 'technically' in the Hungarian army, but to some extent they were controlled by the Ministry for the Interior. As Hungarian army units became involved on the Russian front, these Labour Battalion Jews went with them. But the Hungarian units did not advance for long. The whole 2nd Hungarian Army, including the Labour Battalion units with them, was completely annihilated. This happened at the very spot where the Chernobyl nuclear complex was built years later. Some

250,000 Hungarian soldiers perished, along with approximately 50,000 men in the Jewish Labour Battalions. The Hungarian army used these Jews in the most dangerous places, in mine-clearing for example: the men were just forced to trample through minefields.[19]

HS: Where did the 400 survive?

JC: In Auschwitz, Bochum, Buchenwald and other concentration camps. They survived the deportations.

HS: What happened when the Germans marched into your town?

JC: Györ is situated exactly halfway between Budapest and Vienna, not very far from the Austro-Hungarian border. The German army trucks were speeding through town towards Budapest. We watched them through the windows of our flat. We had two or three relatives in town who had lived through German *blitzkrieg* occupations in other countries. They knew from first-hand experience what was happening. They had gone underground and escaped from Austria and Czechoslovakia to Hungary, and now it was happening again. One lady went underground again, survived the war, but died shortly afterwards.

It was the Hungarian authorities who acted against the Jews, particularly the Hungarian gendarmerie who worked in close collaboration with the Germans. In Hungary there were two types of police – one operated mainly in towns, the other in the country areas. It was not actually quite that simple, but the gendarmerie was very antisemitic, and did the Nazis' 'work' for them. Hungary also had a large Nazi party, the Arrow Cross, who more than just 'assisted' their masters. After the first air raid on the town, we were prohibited from attending school. We had to move into a ghetto which I believe was established on about 25 April 1944. My family was probably luckier than many others who were forced into the ghetto. One of our tradesmen lived in the district designated as the ghetto area. In town my family lived in six or seven different houses, but we all moved into that tradesman's house in the ghetto, and he moved into the main house where our building materials firm was located.

HS: Which members of your family moved into the ghetto?

JC: My parents, my father's brother and sisters, and their families, it was about 35 people altogether.

HS: Did you have any siblings?

JC: No, I was an only child. I can't quite remember the precise number, but about 35 family members moved into our tradesman's house. It was very crowded; it was only a normal-sized house. But we were fortunate to have all the family together. For me personally, those first days were interesting: I was young, 17 years old. I spoke German and the newly established Jewish Council used me as an interpreter and messenger to the SS authorities. To enable me to carry out my tasks, I was allowed to keep my bicycle, and I had a special pass to get out of the ghetto into town, acting on behalf of the Jewish Council. That situation only lasted for about ten days.

HS: Did you learn to speak German in Vienna?

JC: Yes, I spent the first seven years of my life there, and we spoke German at home. When we moved to Hungary in 1934, I spoke no Hungarian at all. Because Hungary was a member of the Axis Pact, German was the first foreign language in schools – no English or French. Obviously, I had no problem with German at school.

HS: You were in the ghetto for ten days only?

JC: No, it was just in the *first* ten days that I could leave the ghetto on my Jewish Council errands. We remained in that ghetto until the middle or end of May 1944. One day we were driven out, strip-searched and all our remaining property was confiscated. We were then taken to the outskirts of town into a larger regional ghetto, where we were accommodated in dilapidated buildings, originally built for Italian prisoners of war during World War I. The buildings had been used in the 1930s by gypsies, but they abandoned them because of the lack of water, electricity and sanitation, yet the Nazis found them good enough to 'house' 6,000 Jews. From there, I was deported to Auschwitz on 11 June 1944. There were over 80 people in each goods wagon, in extremely crowded conditions, for a journey that lasted three days.

Since Györ is so close to the Austrian *(Ostmark)* border, Eichmann's original plan was for our particular trainload of Jews to be taken as 'fodder' to the armament factories near Vienna. The train's SS escort was so used to taking all transports to Auschwitz that the train was already approaching the Carpathian mountains before they discovered their mistake. After hurried communications, Eichmann instructed his team to take our transport to Auschwitz, saying that "the next load can then go to the *Ostmark*". And that is what happened. The next transport, from Szeged in a completely different part of Hungary, really did go to Wiener Neustadt. That transport included my only surviving cousin, who survived near Vienna with her then two-year-old daughter, her mother-in-law and most of the others deported on that train. My surviving niece now lives in Switzerland. These are my only relatives who survived. All 58 other family members perished in Auschwitz.[20] Our transport arrived in Auschwitz-Birkenau on 15 or 16 June 1944.

HS: Were you the only member of your family on that transport?

JC: No, the whole family – or most of them – was on that first train. Of our family, only my father, my uncle and I survived the initial selection on the ramp. The three of us were taken into the Auschwitz-Birkenau camp, but all the rest of the family were gassed. This was in mid-June 1944. Before being taken as slave labourers for the German armament industry, we had to undergo a selection for the so-called *Arbeitskommandos* (work-groups). We were in Birkenau until mid-August and during our time there, one night the SS gassed and murdered all 26,000 gypsies in the camp. On 20 August 1944, we were taken in a transport of 270 men to Bochum in Westphalia.

HS: Did you and your father manage to stay together?

JC: Yes, somehow we did. My uncle stayed in Auschwitz (Birkenau). He was in another barracks, on the other side of the barbed wire fence. We occasionally managed to communicate with each other across the wire. The last news I had of him was that he was still alive in Birkenau in November 1944.

HS: I could check in Auschwitz, if you like, to see whether the records say anything about him.

JC: His first name was István and he was born about 1887. Of course, I don't know what age he gave to the camp authorities. As you know, many older people changed their birthdates to give the impression that they were younger, thus improving their chances of being considered fit for work as *Depotjuden*. My father, who was actually born in 1896, gave 1902 as his year of birth. I myself, born in 1927, made myself older by giving 1924 as my birthdate.

HS: It's rather unlikely that we'll find anything about your uncle. So many transports were arriving at the end of November 1944 that things were rather chaotic in Birkenau. The last transports from Terezin and the other camps came at the end of October. Most of these prisoners were not even registered. Those who survived the 'selections' were put in the so-called 'Transit Camp' and then transported to work elsewhere – just as you were earlier in 1944. It's possible that your uncle was sent to another work camp even later.[21]

JC: Here is a story that will probably interest you. When we arrived in Auschwitz in mid-June 1944, a transport from Luxembourg also came in at about the same time. As we were in the same barracks, I became friendly with a young man from Luxembourg who came on that transport; he was about my age, and was very 'lost' and alone. A few years ago I spoke to an Auschwitz survivor who was from Luxembourg. He found out about the transport in question and the young man I mentioned. It turned out that my 'friend' was one of about a dozen people who survived the initial selection on arrival. He had been taken from a special hospital in Luxembourg and was mentally handicapped. But that's another story!

HS: You were a young man when you arrived in Bochum, but your father was much older. You were in the camp in the Brüllstrasse. Did you have any contact with the local people, at least at your workplace? Can you tell me something about it?

JC: Very little. I worked in the armament works of the *Bochumer Verein*. It was so hot and noisy that hardly any Germans worked there.

HS: What sort of plant was it?

JC: It was a foundry and forge-press plant. Most people working there were Jewish slave labourers, and there were also a few Poles and Russians.[22] There was no contact with the German people. We had two or three German foremen. My foreman used to hit and thump us all the time. Sometimes he gave us potato peelings to eat – that was his 'good' side. The only time we had any contact with the local people was during air raids, when we were in the cellar. Even there, we had to keep to a designated corner of the shelter.

HS: What was the accommodation like in the Brüllstrasse camp?

JC: Every morning, we had to march to the factory, then do twelve hours' hard labour with a half-hour meal break. Before we set off, there was of course a roll-call, which took half an hour or so. Then it was a half-hour march to the factory for our twelve-hour shift. Then we had to march back to the camp, and after yet another roll-call, we just fell into our bunks, utterly exhausted. We were housed in barracks, subdivided into four or five rooms, with about 50 people in each room. Not all the barracks were the same size. The camp was hit in air raids and afterwards only half or two-thirds of the barracks remained useable. As far as I recall, the same number of prisoners just had to crowd into less space.

HS: Did you receive proper nourishment?

JC: Yes, if you can call it 'proper'. Our normal, daily food was thin, very watery cabbage soup, 200 grammes of bread, a little synthetic margarine, some seaweed or something similar twice a week, and one cigarette a week. We also received some 'Camp Money'. What value it had is anybody's guess. I certainly didn't become a millionaire!

HS: The food was inadequate and the work very heavy. What effect did this have on you and your fellow prisoners in the barracks?

JC: Before the German occupation, we had had a relatively good life in Hungary. Food was far more plentiful than in Germany – or England. So our bodies had quite a bit of 'tactical reserves'. But of course, after the ghetto, Auschwitz, then Bochum and the heavy work, all these reserves had disappeared.

HS: You lost your father in December. Did you say he died a natural death?

JC: Yes, he did. The camp authorities always registered 'heart failure' or something similar as the cause of death, no matter what the real reason was. In my father's case, it really was natural causes. Of course, he was very emaciated.

HS: Was he with you in the barracks?

JC: No, in his last days he was moved from his barrack bunk to a sort of sick bay. That is where he died.

HS: Mr Chillag, my questions are obviously upsetting. You don't have to answer them, if you don't want to.

JC: Carry on. I would like to answer all your questions, and tell you everything.

HS: You and your father were the last remaining survivors of your family, so it was an extremely traumatic situation.

JC: Yes, it was a very difficult time, but with the heavy work, the exhaustion, the camp, there was no time to think. I really can't remember my feelings in detail: nature has its mental block.

HS: Was there ever any hope of getting out of there?

JC: Hope? Yes, perhaps. We had been forced to leave Hungary just a few days after D-Day, after the Normandy invasion took place. So we knew that the final battles of the war had begun. In December 1944, or perhaps just a few days after my father died, you could hear artillery fire in the distance. We had no other news. Occasionally we saw bits of German newspapers, but knew they would not print the truth of the real situation.

HS: Let's talk a bit about Hans Satler.[23]

JC: Hans Satler arrived in the Brüllstrasse camp in Bochum about the same time as me. We were amongst the youngest prisoners there. We worked in the same 'hall', possibly for most of the time we were there. He worked on the gantry crane which lifted the heavy forgings. It was very hard work. He worked above the presses and I worked below. One day we hatched a scheme that he would slowly lower the hoist onto my toes. I hoped my toes would be slightly squashed so I could then be off work and in the sick bay for a few days. It didn't quite work out like that: the toe wasn't just squashed, it was broken. But that was my good fortune. The toe was put in plaster and I had to be off work for three weeks. It probably meant the difference between my survival or death.

HS: Do you know anything else about Hans Satler?

JC: I've never met anyone who spoke such beautiful clear German as Hans. No trace of any accent; no trace of Prussian, Bavarian, or *Ruhr-Deutsch*, just the purest '*Hoch-Deutsch*'. He came to Bochum from the ghetto in Riga, but he wasn't from there originally. He had been deported to Riga with many other German Jews in 1942 – I don't know where from. Then he was brought back to Germany as a slave labourer. By the way, about ten years ago I heard from a Jew from Gelsenkirchen, who was also taken back on the same slave labour transport from Riga to Bochum. I've forgotten his name.

HS: That is Herr Abrahamson.[24] He survived and later became the chairman of the Jewish community of 'Bochum-Herne-Recklinghausen'. That story is grotesque: the Riga ghetto was cleared of indigenous Jews to make room for Jews from Germany. A transport of Bochum Jews was taken to Riga in January 1942. And in 1944 Jews were brought back as slave labourers from Riga to Bochum. When did you lose contact with Hans Satler? According to our information, he died on 10 January 1945.

JC: We were still together when my injured toe healed, but I can't remember much more. He was in a different barracks, possibly one adjacent to mine. I probably wouldn't have remembered him at all, but the VVN booklet and the picture of the gravestone with his name brought it all back to me.

HS: Mr Chillag, you were then taken to Buchenwald?

JC: Yes, I was taken to Buchenwald along with about 1,300 other prisoners, on the last transport evacuating the inmates. In my recent research in Buchenwald, I discovered that we left Bochum on 21 March 1945 and arrived in Buchenwald two days later.

HS: Can you recall this journey? What do you remember?

JC: There was increasing artillery fire, so we realised that the front was getting closer. Of the journey itself – if you can call it a journey – I can't remember much. I was too weak.

HS: Was it a goods train?

JC: It must have been a train, but whether it was a goods train, with closed or open wagons, or a passenger train, I really can't remember.

HS: I can imagine how depressed you must all have been with this torture continuing…

JC: Yes, but by that time I was so weak that I was past caring. Today I can imagine what it must have been like, but at the time I couldn't think at all. I was semi-conscious. When we got to Buchenwald, I was taken to the so-called 'Small Camp'. It was a Sick-Camp, next to the crematorium – logistically convenient for the 'final journey'. How I survived those last days – two weeks – I just don't know. I was too weak to get down from the bunk, I was wedged in the middle of three or four people. I was 18 years old. I could not get down to go to the toilet; we had to go where we were. And it poured down on us as well from the bunks above.

HS: You lived through the liberation of Buchenwald, then I think you stayed there for a while until you had been nursed back to 'life'?

JC: Yes, initially – not just me, but most of the others who were extremely weak and sick. The Americans arrived. Their soldiers were emptying their pockets and distributing chewing gum, chocolate bars, meat and so on. Many of the liberated prisoners just gulped all this down. Their systems couldn't absorb this 'food' and many lost their lives as a result. I was protected from all this; I was lying in my bunk, far too weak even to reach out for the 'goodies'. Then medical teams arrived and we were transferred into buildings previously occupied by the SS, which were turned into field hospitals.

HS: How long did you stay there ?

JC: I was there until the Americans withdrew from the area (which became part of the Soviet occupation zone) – until the middle of July, or so. In my final days there, I was strong enough to supervise a group of local Germans loading trucks. The Americans were removing everything from the factories around Buchenwald – machinery, equipment, documentation, etc. I was there until just before the Russians took over the area.

HS: What was happening in Buchenwald then?

JC: Former prisoners could leave the camp. Many were returning to their home countries, to France, and so on. Not all those from East European countries – Hungary, Czechoslovakia and Poland – wanted to return to their former homes because of political developments and uncertainties there. Most Russians didn't want to go back, but were repatriated to the Soviet Union by force. I wanted to return to Györ. I thought someone from the family would have survived. In the event, no one had survived, but I didn't know that at the time. In mid-July, the Americans took me to Czechoslovakia on one of the last trucks to leave, and they organised a special train to take us back to Hungary. It was a very long and slow journey because all military transport had priority and the railway track was damaged. On the journey we stopped for three hours at a small village where one of my uncles and his family had lived before the German occupation. I went into the village to see whether they had survived. Alas, they had not. The train eventually reached Budapest, then a few days later I travelled on to Györ. My initial hopes of finding any family survivors were soon dashed. Not a single family member deported from Györ survived. With a heavy heart, I started to rebuild the family business, together with the husband of my cousin (the one

26

who survived in Wiener Neustadt). He had been in a Labour Battalion for three years, and that was where he survived the Nazi period. We ran the business until it was nationalised by the Communists in 1949. Shortly after that, I emigrated to Australia.

HS: Australia? Was that planned or by chance?

JC: It was by chance in that I was applying for visas to go to the USA, Canada and Australia, and the visa for Australia came first.

HS: Mr Chillag, before we talk further about your life on your return to Hungary, I would like to ask you about something else. I myself know many survivors of Jewish origin and often talk with them. These people also have a need to talk. But my experience is almost always that the survivors, now mostly in their late seventies, have kept silent about this period in their lives for decades; they have not even spoken to their children about it. Do you think it's perhaps because they don't want to burden their children, or they are perhaps afraid their children may not be interested?

JC: I am not a psychologist. It was some 40 years before my own trauma lifted. Some people say that it is because films like *Shoah* or *Schindler's List* opened the floodgates. But in my own case, it actually happened before these films were screened. I just don't know why we were unable to talk about these events immediately after the war, but now almost everybody can. Perhaps in order to carry on with life, we had to push these horrors out of the way.

HS: Mr Chillag, may I ask a few questions about your life after surviving? What was the situation in Győr when you returned there in August 1945?

JC: I first spent a few days in Budapest with distant relatives and friends who had survived the Nazi and Arrow Cross period there with a Swiss or Swedish '*Schutz Pass.*'[25] After that, I continued my journey to Györ. There was a welfare office for returned deportees, and I had already been told in Budapest that I should go to this office, which was in the grounds of the synagogue. There I met a dozen or so other survivors who had returned to the town. They gave me information about who else had survived, where I could get assistance, and so on. After spending a few hours in this office, I gathered enough courage to walk to my family's former main house, the location of the family business before the deportations. Half of it had been destroyed by bombs, and the building yard was completely flattened. Russian soldiers were billeted in the remainder of the house. Just one room was still occupied by our former tradesman – the one we had 'swapped' houses with when we had to move into the ghetto. He was an old Socialist and was welcoming enough, but he had no control over the house, so I couldn't move back in. Next, I went to the house where my parents and I used to live. There the reception I got was really hostile. Not one piece of our furniture was in the house; the new occupants were protégés of the Russians and Communist party, so there was no chance of reclaiming the accommodation.

In the end, I finished up living in the only undamaged basement room of the family house. I was living there when my relative – my cousin's husband – arrived. We tried to rebuild the family business, and were helped by a few non-Jewish family friends and a handful of people from the town. The rest of Györ's population, while not positively hostile and resentful, was anything but helpful towards the returned deportees.

An amusing event took place shortly after my return. I was summoned to the local Communist party headquarters. The party secretary, who had gone into political exile in Vienna in 1920 along with my father, called me in to enquire about him. He offered to help me, but nothing transpired. This party secretary was Zoltán Szántó, later ambassador to

Tito, who was incarcerated during the trials of the Hungarian Deputy-Premier Rajk and executed after the Hungarian Uprising in 1956.

HS: When you returned, your school education was incomplete. Did this make your new start difficult?

JC: Yes, it did. Before we were forced into the ghetto, I was 17 and about to finish 7th Grade in grammar school. I should have taken my final examination in June 1945. As the Hungarian front moved westwards, many of my teachers fled westwards too – some were very bad teachers, but good Arrow Cross members. A few exceptionally capable teachers helped four returned students from my year – I was the only Jew who came back – to take an 'accelerated' course towards matriculation (the final examination). I obtained good results and could have gone to university the next day. But how could I? I was in the process of rebuilding the family business and somehow I had to earn a living as well.

HS: Was there anything else that you could do? What were the difficulties you encountered?

JC: The building, sheds and storerooms were all in ruins. All the stock had been plundered long before my return. Efforts to get government assistance came to very little. Before I left Buchenwald, I had found some Hungarian pengö currency in a rubbish heap.[26] In spite of the galloping inflation in Hungary, this money was still enough to buy our first goods wagon of cement for the business. Building materials for reconstruction were in great demand. Rebuilding the business was hard work, but it was not all that difficult. Black-market methylated spirits also helped. A sufficient quantity 'encouraged' the Russian soldiers to leave the premises. My cousin was then able to move into the vacated house with his family. Another 200 litres of the stuff 'bought' us a truck.

Not long afterwards, the (by then) Communist regime confiscated and nationalised the business. Almost at the same time, I received my call-up papers for the Hungarian army. With my father's political background from 1919 onwards and the time I had spent in the concentration camps, I was regarded as sufficiently 'reliable' and linguistically suitable to serve in an elite radio reconnaissance unit (the equivalent of today's SIGINT: Signals Intelligence, in the West). Many men serving in this army unit were involved in the 1956 uprising and lost their lives then. Some of the senior officers were executed after show trials.

I didn't want anything to do with the army. Using most of the capital I had left, I managed to bribe myself out and get a year's postponement of my military service. After the business was nationalised, I started planning my escape from Hungary.

HS: Did you have a specific destination in mind? And what were the chances of escaping?

JC: I planned my escape with a childhood friend who had survived Mauthausen, his girlfriend and three men who had survived in Budapest, and we also had a guide. We all emigrated to Australia eventually – although on different ships.

We knew that by 1949 escaping to Austria through barbed wire and minefields was far too dangerous. So we took a train to the opposite end of Hungary, to Miskolc in the north-east. There we climbed over the mountains into Slovakia, took another train to Bratislava, and then crossed the Austrian border on foot. It wasn't easy, but we managed it without too many difficulties.

When we were already over the border in Austria, Russian soldiers discovered us and chased us. (Austria was still under four-power occupation then.) We managed to reach Vienna, but only felt safe when we had reached the American Zone. In Vienna we found refuge in the 'Rotschild Hospital', the centre operated by the 'Joint' (AJDC)[27] to help the Jewish refugees pouring in from Eastern Europe. This was the staging post for some 2,000-3,000 people as they emigrated to Israel, the USA, Australia and so on. Until they reached their final destination, their subsistence expenses were paid in most cases by the Joint. I was in Vienna from 20 August 1949 until mid-February 1950, when I was taken in an American military convoy across to Steyr in the American Zone. A few weeks later, my papers for Australia arrived and I set off by train for embarkation at an Italian port. En route, we stopped at two or three places, and many more railway coaches were added on to our train, filled with hundreds of Displaced Persons.[28] Our special train crossed the Brenner Pass and we disembarked in Senigallia. After a few days in the transit camp there, we were taken via Aversa to Bagnoli near Naples. The huge camp in Bagnoli was a Balilla Academy (Members of the Fascist Youth Movement) during the Mussolini era. Each of the dormitories there housed 500-600 people, all waiting for various ships to take them to their destinations. After two weeks there, 1,200 of the DPs embarked on a US Navy ship, *'General M.B. Stewart'*, for our sea journey to Australia.

HS: Let's try to clarify something. How did one become a DP, a Displaced Person? And how was the transportation of these groups organised to the 'destination countries'?

JC: First of all I need to point out that in 1947, in addition to the 160,000 Jewish Displaced Persons, there were about half a million non-Jewish Displaced Persons in camps. In 1949, there was another much smaller wave of Jewish refugees from Eastern Europe. They were fleeing from new antisemitic outbursts and from political 'takeovers'. These Jews came mainly from Hungary, Rumania, Poland and Czechoslovakia. This group, which included people like me, had to wait in holding

31

camps in Austria and Germany, or in other transit countries. The preparatory work to transport these people to a final destination was in the hands of UNRRA/IRO,[29] an agency of the United Nations. It operated under the usual parameters of the UN Charter, with conditions to comply with the standard philosophy (still applying to this day!): no aid or relief for economic migrants.

I have already mentioned that in 1949 there were still a large number of residual non-Jewish Displaced Persons in German and Austrian camps remaining from wartime. These ranged from ethnic Germans (*Volksdeutsche*), willing or coerced *Ostarbeiter* (forced labourers from occupied Polish and Soviet territories), to soldiers and civilians from former East Europe, among them probable war criminals and politicians of dubious character. Some had no wish to return to the 'East', others – perhaps for good reason – feared for their lives if they returned. Yet others were still plotting the overthrow of the regimes from which they had fled. With the exception of this last group, all the other Displaced Persons were hoping to emigrate to the West, or to settle permanently in Germany or Austria. To be accepted for emigration, certain conditions had to be checked, met and verified by the IRO along the lines of: country X would be willing to accept person Y, subject to good health, certain vocational qualifications and a 'clean' political and criminal record. The political checks were mostly superficial and many people of rather dubious character slipped through the net. Once the checking process was complete for, say, 1,500 people to the same destination, the IRO and immigration staff from the prospective host country got together to do the necessary preparatory work – to arrange transport to a port, charter of ships and all the other logistics. From that point on, the future host country took over responsibility for the prospective immigrants – for land and sea transportation, food, protection and work opportunities, and the financial burden was shared between the UN and host country.

HS: And how did you become accepted as a 'Displaced Person'?

JC: I mentioned that 'economic refugees' were not eligible for IRO assistance. And guess what? The IRO automatically considered all Jewish refugees from East Europe as 'economic refugees', particularly because they knew that the Jews who had fled had a 'fairy godmother': the Joint. Nevertheless, whenever the Joint thought one of its Jewish protégés stood a chance of being classed as 'political', it tried to put this 'political refugee' through the IRO selection process. The IRO interview panel in Vienna which investigated and checked these candidates was chaired by a Hungarian fascist landowner who had fled from the Russians in April 1945. Not surprisingly, in the six months I spent in Vienna, of the thousands of Jewish applicants, I believe only eight succeeded in receiving an IRO Passport!

HS: This questionable process must have been very depressing for people like you. And I can imagine that a selection process like this also reflected on the type of immigrant accepted for Australia....

JC: Of course. In a nutshell, it was a very mixed bunch. About a quarter of them came from Trieste, and they included many Croats, Serbs and people from other Yugoslav ethnic groups. The American military police aboard the ship had a difficult job separating these groups from each other, trying to prevent disputes and even knifings. The next largest group was from the Baltic countries, some with very dubious wartime backgrounds. Other DP passengers included Hungarian ex-army officers, some of them quite boastful of their Arrow Cross past, as well as Poles, Russians, Ukrainians and a few Czechs. Our ship, the *'General M.B. Stewart'* had a US navy crew and Malaysian cooks. Accommodation was in large dormitories, with men and women separated on different decks. I was lucky. By embarking in Naples with an advance party, a young

Czech DP and I were given the task of producing a newspaper for our fellow passengers. The main benefit was that the two of us shared an office on board – which was also our cabin for the journey. Eating in the Navy mess, we also got better food. The main excitement aboard ship throughout the passage to Sydney was the constant fights, mainly between the Yugoslav factions. We arrived in Sydney on 17 April 1950, and were taken by train to a reception camp for 'New Australians' near the city of Bathurst, some 250 km west of Sydney – 'in the middle of nowhere' .

HS: Mr Chillag, you say 'in the middle of nowhere'? That doesn't sound very optimistic. Were you not made welcome in Australia? You remained there for many years. How did you finally integrate? Did you become a 'real' fair-dinkum Aussie?

JC: The main condition for DPs admitted to Australia under the IRO scheme was that 'New Australians', as we were officially called, (although more often than not we were referred to as 'Refos', 'Balts', 'Wogs', or just 'bloody foreigners'), had to work for two years in 'directed' employment, wherever they were sent by the Government Employment Service. This rule, incidentally, did not apply to people arriving under the auspices of the 'Joint'.

Bathurst is about the coldest place there is in Australia, with hard frost in April, the Australian autumn. To live in the camp there, in a tent, waiting for an employment offer, was no fun at all. So after a few days in the camp, I ventured into Bathurst and took the first train to Sydney. I very quickly noticed that Australian English is very different from English English! At that time my English was inadequate anyway: I couldn't understand a single word the locals were saying, nor could they make any sense of my so-called English. Anyway, I did get to Sydney, where I went to the employment office and was directed to a job in a foundry, making bolts and screws. (Presumably my training from my *Bochumer Verein* days stood me in good stead!)

Shift work gave me the freedom to get involved in other activities. I mixed with the local Australians and learnt the language faster than most other migrants. I enrolled in college to get a qualification in building construction (although I had to give up this course a year later). After about a year, I changed my job – and went to make chicken noodle soup for Nestlés. About this time I sat and passed the 'Public Service Entrance Examination', which opened up new and better perspectives than the manual labour I had so far been doing.

With my new certificate, I applied for a position with the Snowy Mountains Authority (SMA), one of the largest hydro-electric projects in the world. Soon I was to start working on their first dam and power station, testing concrete in the materials laboratory. So for the first time since leaving Hungary, I was back in the construction materials business!

The SMA was a melting pot for full integration into Australian life. People from over 50 nations worked on that project. There were the main Norwegian and American contractors, migrants from the UK, pre- and post-war refugees, Displaced Persons of many nationalities, and – perhaps surprisingly – a large number of Australians too. There were also a number of politically 'clean' German engineers, surveyors and so on, including a number of ex-Afrika Corps and *Wehrmacht* (German army) technicians who had been recruited by the SMA in Germany.

On the Snowy project, at Island Bend, I met my future wife, who worked in the office at the dam site. Six months later, we got married in a church which today lies 50 metres under the water of a huge storage reservoir. We worked there for five years, the last year in the central laboratory in Cooma. Five years after my arrival in Australia, I became an Australian citizen.

The time we spent 'on top' of Australia in the Snowy Mountains near Mt. Kosciusko, with its cold, dry climate and lots of snow and skiing, suited us fine. But Cooma was a very bureaucratic and class-divided place. Our two sons had been born by then and we decided to move to Sydney. In Australia in those days, paper qualifications were far less important than natural ability. Based on my past experience, I was offered a position in the engineering laboratories of the Australian Atomic Energy Commission. I moved from concrete to metals and nuclear materials. This was a position in a high security establishment, so there were hardly any ex-migrants working there. I became and regarded myself as a fully assimilated and integrated Aussie.

HS: Mr Chillag, at the end of this interview I would like to raise an issue which is currently on everyone's minds – 'compensation'. I know the idea of compensation is totally inadequate for the suffering endured, and your own experience only confirms this. But is it something you have ever considered?

JC: Yes. I did once try to claim compensation. It was in the early 1960s and I made a claim for 'injury to life'. The Frankfurt law firm of Dr Robert Kempner[30] and R I Levin submitted the claim on my behalf. It was rejected. This is a translation of the letter Mr Levin wrote to me on 27 November 1963, paraphrasing the dismissal of the claim:

> Dear Mr Chillag,
> Referring to your claim for compensation on grounds of 'Injury to Life', we regret to inform you that the Compensation Adjudication Authority in Mainz has dismissed your claim.
> Compensation on grounds of 'Injury to Life' can normally only be paid to persons up to the age of 18, which you had already reached in 1945. However, compensation can be paid beyond this age to orphans who are undergoing school education or vocational training. Claimants in your category can claim payment of an orphan's allowance from 1.1.1949, provided that the legal requirements for this allowance are met from that date. In your case, a judgement had to be made as to whether on the critical

date of 1.1.1949 you were still in school education or professional/ vocational training. The Authority is of the opinion that you were not. The grounds are as follows:

'The claimant gave proof of vocational training up to 3.10.1946. On becoming a craftsman, he was employed until 31.10.1948... Following his emigration in February 1950, he was, according to his own statement, employed from May 1950 to May 1952 as a labourer, and then as a laboratory assistant until March 1957. Attendance for further education at the British Institute of Engineering Technology does not constitute 'vocational training' as defined in the Employee Remuneration Act.

...The claimant not having met the stipulations of para.7 of the 1st DV-BEG beyond 1.1.1949, the claim for payment of an 'orphan's allowance' is dismissed.

You will notice that the dismissal of the claim hinges on the finding that attendance at the British Institute does not constitute full-time professional training, as apparently this was a correspondence course (cf. your letter of 2.10.1963).

An appeal would have to be submitted to the Court. However, as things stand, we fear that there is no chance of success, and can only recommend that you do not go ahead with an appeal.

However, should you be able to prove your claim against the Authority's findings, ie. that you were in full-time professional training after 1.1.1949, you may wish to appeal. And we would also remind you of the deadline for such an appeal.

HS: Mr Chillag, This conversation was obviously very difficult for you. Many thanks indeed for your cooperation.

Dr Hubert Schneider, born 1941, historian at the Ruhr-University Bochum (RUB) and chairman of "Remembering for the Future" Association, Bochum. His recent publications are on the history of the Bochum Jewish community.

Appendix

Members of the Csillag (now Chillag) Family who perished in the Holocaust

Perished in Concentration and Extermination Camps	Perished in Labour Battalions, on death marches, on the Russian front or elsewhere
József CSILLAG, my father, an accountant (died: Bochumer Verein Auxiliary Slave labour camp – KL Buchenwald, Bochum 5.12.1944)	
Aranka CSILLAG (Mayer), my mother: Dressmaker (Auschwitz 1944)	
Dr. Sándor POLGÁR, botanist and teacher, his wife: Margit (Csillag)[A] (Auschwitz, 1944)	and their son: Dr. Ferenc POLGÁR, physician (Labour Battalion, Russian front 1942)
József KEMÉNY, Treasury officer, his wife: Irma (Csillag)[A] (Auschwitz, 1944)	and their sons: Dr. Pál KEMÉNY, mechanical engineer (Labour Battalion) and Zoltán KEMÉNY, textile engineer (Labour Battalion, Bor)
Dr. Ödön FÜLÖP, miller and lawyer, his wife Böske (Chillag)[A] and their children: Ella (Fülöp), her husband: Oszkár MANDL and their son Péter	

Perished in Concentration and Extermination Camps	Perished in Labour Battalions, on death marches, on the Russian front or elsewhere
Ágnes, (Fülöp), her husband: Dr László HAÁSZ, paediatrician, and their children: Miklós and Judit Éva (Fülöp) FAZEKAS, journalist, and her son János (all Auschwitz 1944)	
István CSILLAG[A], merchant and businessman (Auschwitz Nov.? 1944)	and his son: Palkó CSILLAG (Labour Battalion, Russian front 1942)
Edit CSILLAG (Halász), child psychologist (Auschwitz 1944) and their daughter: Annuska (Auschwitz 1944)	and her husband: Dr. György CSILLAG[B], physician, (Labour Battalion, Russian front 1942)
Jenö CSILLAG[B], railway engineer, his wife Jolán (Naményi), (Auschwitz 1944) their children: Magda (Csillag) KRAUSZ, and her children Márta and Ferike (Auschwitz 1944)	and Bandi CSILLAG, (Magda's brother) (Labour Battalion, Russian front 1942)
Laci STEINER[B] and his wife Elza (Lamm) (Auschwitz 1944)	and their son: Hans-Péter STEINER, (death marches, 1945)
	Gyula CSILLAG, (death marches, 1945)
Artur CSILLAG[B], land agent, and his wife Ida (Kohn), their daughter Bözsi and her child (Auschwitz 1944)	and their son: Alajos CSILLAG (Labour Battalion, Russian front 1943)

Perished in Concentration and Extermination Camps	Perished in Labour Battalions, on death marches, on the Russian front or elsewhere
Béla CSILLAG[B], and his wife Berta, (Auschwitz 1944)	and their son: Imre CSILLAG (Labour Battalion, Russian front 1942)
Heda CSILLAG[C] (Hönigstein), oil merchant, (Auschwitz, June 1944)	and her son: Imre CSILLAG, (Labour Battalion, Russian front 1942)
Ernesztine CSILLAG* (Steiner) (Auschwitz 1944)	
Jenö SOMLÓ[B] and his wife Margit (Takács) (Auschwitz 1944)	
György STEINER[B] and his wife Ella (Auschwitz 1944)	
Imre STEINER[B] and his wife Margit (Krausz) (Auschwitz 1944)	
Pali STEINER[B] and his wife Ibolya, (Auschwitz 1944)	
Jenö SZABÓ[C], textile merchant (Auschwitz 1944)	
Dr. József TAKÁCS[B], physician, his wife Ella (Schwartz), and their daughter Vera (Auschwitz 1944)	
Helén MAYER (Duschinsky)[D], (Auschwitz 1944)	
her son: Sanyi MAYER[E], textile engineer,	
and his son Ervin, (Auschwitz 1944)	

[A] my father's sister/brother
[C] spouse of my father's cousin
[E] my maternal uncle, cousin

[B] my father's cousin
[D] my maternal grandmother
* my father's aunt

Notes

1. John Chillag, who now lives in Great Britain, was born Johann Paul Csillag in Vienna in 1927. Throughout this account, his name will appear as John Chillag, the form of the name he now uses.

2. The history of the cemetery is described in great detail in M. Keller and G. Wilbertz, *Spuren im Stein: Ein Bochumer Friedhof als Spiegel jüdischer Geschichte* (KlartexVerlag, Essen, 1997), from which this information is taken.

3. *Die Verfolgung der Juden in Bochum und Wattenscheid. Die Jahre 1933-1945 in Berichten, Bildern und Dokumenten.* VVN Bund der Antifaschisten (Publishers), Altenberg, 1993. All translations from German documents are my own.

4. D. Czech, *Auschwitz Chronicle 1939–1945*, I. B. Tauris, London, 1990.

5. *Auschwitz Chronicle*, p. 58.

6. *Auschwitz Chronicle*, p. 645.

7. *Auschwitz Chronicle*, p. 692.

8. Details of this 'paper transaction' appear on a list of names dated 31.10.1944 produced by the Political Department of KZ Buchenwald: *Neuzugänge vom 31.Okt.1944: 270 Häftlinge von KL Auschwitz nach Arb.Kdo.Bochum – eingetroffen am 21. Aug.1944.* Copy held by the *Erinnern für die Zukunft e.V. Association*, Bochum. The original is in the archives of the *Gedenkstätte* Buchenwald.

9. Hans Frankenthal, a survivor of Auschwitz concentration and extermination camp, returned after the Liberation to his home town of Schmallenberg. He became involved in the renewal of Jewish life in post-war Germany and the so-called 'Compensation' issue. Shortly before his death in December 1999, his memoirs were published, entitled *Verweigerte Rückkehr – Erfahrungen nach dem Judenmord*, dealing not only with Frankenthal's childhood and adolescence in Schmallenberg, his suffering in Auschwitz-Monowitz, but also with the difficulties he experienced as a Jew in post-1945 Germany.

10. This letter and all the documents cited hereafter are held in the archives of the *Erinnern für die Zukunft e.V. Association*, Bochum.

11. The extensive literature available on the subject includes: A. Biss, *Der Stopp der Entlösung. Kampf gegen Hitler und Eichmann in Budapest*, Stuttgart, 1966; R. L. Braham (ed), *The Destruction of Hungarian Jewry* (2 vols), New York, 1963; R. L. Braham and B. Vágó (eds), *The Holocaust in Hungary. Forty Years Later*, New York, 1985; R. L. Braham, *The Hungarian Jewish Catastrophe* (2nd ed) New York, 1984; R. L. Braham, *The Politics of Genocide: The Holocaust in Hungary*, Irvington, 1991; J. S. Conway, "Der Holocaust in Ungarn", in *Vierteljahreshefte für Zeitgeschichte* 32 (1984) 179-202; R. Fischer,

41

Entwicklungstufen des Antisemitismus in Ungarn 1867-1939. Die Zerstörung der Magyarisch-Jüdischen Symbiose, München, 1988; J. Lévai (ed.), *Eichmann in Hungary. Documents*, Budapest, 1961.

12. The life and working conditions of Hungarian Jews in the labour battalions are very graphically described in the autobiography of Béla Zsolt: *Nine Suitcases*, London, 2004.

13. See also the autobiography of Béla Zsolt, endnote 12.

14. Edmund Veesenmayer, the German plenipotentiary for Hungary, gives a figure of 437,402 Jews deported.

15. Strasshof was a slave labour camp for Hungarian Jews deported to Austria. It was essentially a transit camp.

16. In these negotiations Zionists tried to 'buy' Jewish lives in exchange for trucks for the German army. See also the book by T. Segev: *Die siebte Million*, Reinbeck, 1995. The subject of very heated debate, mainly in Israel, the book is very critical of the role played by Zionist organisations in attempting to save European Jews from deportation and extermination.

17. József Kemény, *Vázlatok a Györi Zsidóság Történetéböl*, Györ, 1930.

18. István Domán, *A Györi Izraelita Hitközség Története (1930-1947)*, Budapest, 1979.

19. Some male members of the Csillag family lost their lives whilst serving in the Labour Battalions. See their names listed in the Appendix.

20. A list of the 61 members of John Chillag's extended family who perished in Auschwitz, other camps, labour battalions and death marches appears in the Appendix.

21. Research in Auschwitz-Birkenau's archives has shown that the records of *Depotjuden* (Jewish transit prisoners) were not transferred.

22. This was confirmed by Yevgeni Komar (an *Ostarbeiter*, a Ukrainian forced labourer who was in Bochum at the same time and place as John Chillag) when interviewed in Bochum in 1994. Komar also wrote in a letter that he worked on the presses of *Stahlwerk III/ Bochumer Verein* in a mixed group of Hungarian and Polish slave labourers and Soviet prisoners-of-war.

23. Hans Latter 'Satler' was a fellow slave labourer and friend in Bochum. He died there and is one of the 52 victims buried in Wiemelhausen cemetery. In *Die Verfolgung der Juden in Bochum und Wattenscheid. Die Jahre 1933-1945 in Berichten, Bildern und Dokumenten* (VVN Bund der Antifaschisten) p. 63, there is an illustration showing the gravestone with the inscription 'Hans Satler'. After seeing this booklet, John Chillag said that he knew Hans Satler.

24. When John Chillag visited Bochum in November 2000, he met Herr Abrahamson and it emerged that they were both prisoners in the slave labour camp in Bochum's Brüllstrasse at the same time.

25. In July 1944, on the recommendation of the Swedish Branch of the 'World Jewish Congress', supported by the US 'War Refugee Board', the Swedish Foreign Ministry sent Raoul Wallenberg, one of its diplomats to Budapest. This was in an attempt to set up a rescue operation to save 200,000 Jews in the Hungarian capital (the residue of the 437,000 provincial Hungarian Jews already deported to Auschwitz). Following the *coup d'état* of 15 October 1944 and the takeover by the antisemitic, fascist Arrow Cross Party, Wallenberg issued thousands of Swedish *'Schutzpass'* (safe conduct documents) over a period of three months. These passes, signed by the Swedish ambassador, were respected – in most cases – by both Hungarian and German authorities, and offered very real protection for many Jews. Wallenberg was even successful in personally removing and rescuing Jews who were already aboard deportation trains to Auschwitz. An additional safety net created by Wallenberg was the establishment of 'Swedish Protected Houses', offering a safe haven for 15,000 Jews. Other diplomatic missions provided similar passes and protected houses. Wallenberg was arrested by Soviet forces in 1945 and the fate that befell him is unknown to this day. Cf. P. Anger: *With Raoul Wallenberg in Budapest*, New York, 1981; J. Biermann: *Raoul Wallenberg – der verschollene Held*, München, 1983.

26. The pengö was the Hungarian currency between 1925 and 1946.

27. 'Joint' is the abbreviation for American Joint Distribution Committee (AJDC). Founded after World War I, the Joint organised worldwide help for Jewish people suffering from persecution and pogroms. In the Second World War, it concentrated its work on persecuted European Jewry, for example with food distribution and financial support for rescue. After 1945, the AJDC became the most significant aid organisation to help Jewish survivors of the Nazi extermination policy, and even today it is still one of the largest and most important Jewish welfare organisations.

28. Displaced Person, DP: definition used for people who after liberation from the concentration camps at the end of the war, either could not, or did not wish to return to their original home countries. Regarded as 'stateless', they were housed by the Allied powers in Displaced Persons Holding Camps until a final destination could be found for them.

29. The United Nations Relief and Rehabilitation Administration (UNRRA), a United Nations agency for refugees and citizens of liberated countries in Europe and the Far East, was originally set up on 9 November 1945. UNRRA's main aims included aid to economically suffering countries in dire financial situations, unable to afford to import essential food, as well as the provision of assistance to the millions of DPs to help them in their re-settlement or return to their native countries. UNRRA took over total management, the cultural activities and vocational training in the Displaced Persons Camps established after the war, and also supplemented the food provided by the military authorities. Towards the end of 1945, two-thirds of the holding centres and camps in the western zones of Germany, and 75 per cent of all Displaced Persons were under the protection of UNRRA. On 1 July 1947 the Preparatory Commission

for the International Refugee Organisation (IRO) took over responsibility for the 643,000 Displaced Persons in Europe, who up till then had been protected by UNRRA. During 1948 the last of the UNRRA offices in Europe was closed down, so that when John Chillag fled to Vienna, the organisation of DPs was entirely in the hands of the IRO.

30. The lawyer Robert Kempner was born on 17 October 1899 in Freiburg, Breisgau. From 1928 until his dismissal from service in 1933, he served in the Prussian State Service. He emigrated in the same year and in 1939 went to the USA. From 1946 to 1949, he was first the US Prosecutor and later Deputy Chief Prosecutor at the International Military Tribunal in Nuremberg.

Extract from the 'GLOSSARY' (in the German version):

The *Bochumer Verein Gusstahl (BVG)* Brüllstrasse External Camp of KZ Buchenwald:

The *Aussenlager* (Satellite Camp) of the Concentration Camp Buchenwald was established at the Brüllstrasse, Bochum in the summer of 1944. The camp was built in the Brüllstrasse on a site adjacent to the Armaments Forgings Plant (now the location of the 'Environment Park' near the Kohlenstrasse).

The camp was 'opened for business' on 26 July 1944, with the arrival of 434 slave-labourers from Auschwitz via Buchenwald. These prisoners, as well as the next shipment of 270 Hungarian Jews on 20 August, were personally selected on a visit to Auschwitz by the manager of the BVG Forgings Plant: chief engineer Fritz Helling. The August 'transport' from Auschwitz included John Csillag and his father József.

By November 1944, with more transports from Neuengamme and Buchenwald, the Brüllstrasse Camp held 1,659 predominantly Jewish slave-labourers. The *Bochumer Verein* camp was notorious for its gruesome camp and work conditions. The Commandant of the camp was *SS-Obersturmbannführer* Hermann Grossmann: after the war he was tried by an Allied Military Court, found guilty of heinous war crimes, sentenced to death and executed in Landsberg.

Illustrations

Great-great-grandparents Lipót and Babette Steiner (left) and Jacob and Katalin Förstner (right).
Grandparents of my paternal grandmother Lujza Csillag. Oil painting c. 1840.

My grandfather, Pál Csillag. Photo c. 1905.   *My grandmother, Lujza Csillag (née Steiner).*
                                                  Photo c. 1940.

Arpád u.55, Györ, home and business premises of my grandparents.

1770 Census of Jews in the County of Pozsony (Hungary), with entry for Lázár Majer, my maternal great-great-grandfather.

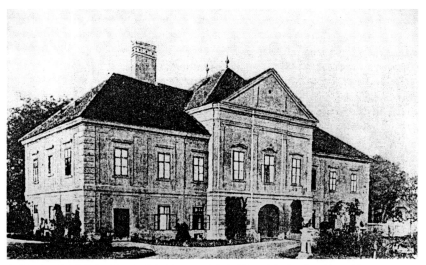

'Fehér Kastély' ('White Mansion') in Dunaszerdahely / Dunajska Streda. (Part of it was my maternal grandparents' flat from 1895 to 1944).

My parents, shortly after their marriage in 1922.

My father, aged 16, in 1912.

Myself in Vienna, 1932, (main), and in Payerbach, 1933, (inset).

48

My mother, 1935, and my father, 1940.

The Révai Gimnázium, my grammar school in Györ.

The first wave of German occupation troops through Györ, 19 March 1944.
(Photo taken in front of my uncle's transport enterprise.)

The railway sidings and crematoria, Auschwitz-Birkenau.

Selection of Hungarian Jews, on the 'Ramp', Auschwitz, June 1944.

Map of my 'Odyssey'.

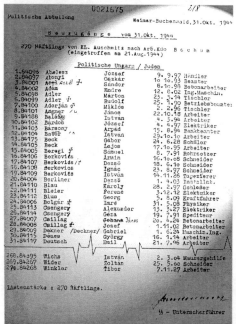

'Neuzugänge' Transfer list from
Auschwitz to Bochum. The list includes
my father and me.

Bochumer Verein and its 'monster'
forge press.

Overview of the Bochumer Verein complex.

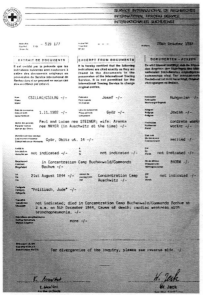

Red Cross Tracing Service response.

Facsimile of Bochum SS Commandant's
teletype message to Buchenwald.

Audrey, my wife, visits my father's grave in the row of 'war' graves at the Bochum Jewish cemetery.
My father's grave and gravestone (inset).

The Infirmary Block, Small Camp, Buchenwald.

Official camp record 'mug-shot'.

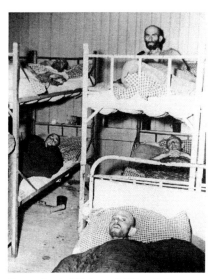

Recovering in US Army field hospital, Buchenwald, (Myself, centre right).

Ausweis — Certification.
Anstatt Reisepass Provisional Pass

János   Csillag

Herr
Mister

geb. am 20.4.1927   Wien
born   Györ

zuletzt wohnhaft
last domicile Opitz Ferenc u. 14

wurde von 14.7.944   bis 11. April 1945

in nationalsozialistischen Konzentrationslagern gefangen
gehalten und vom Konzentrationslager Buchenwald
bei Weimar in Freiheit gesetzt.
                14.7.944
was kept in captivity from   to
in Nazi-German concentrationcamps and was liberated from the
concentrationcamp of Buchenwald.

Unterschriften und Stempel
Government

Lager-Co...
Camp-Co...   Military Lagerkommandant
                Campcommandant

Weimar-Buchenwald, am

Provisional identification card
for civilian internee of Buchenwald.
Vorläufige Identitätskarte für Buchenwälder Zivilinternierte.

Current number 19014   Internee number 84007
Laufende Nr.   Häftlings-Nr.

Family name .... Csillag
Familienname

Christian name .... János
Vorname

Born 20.4.1927   at Wien
geboren   in

Nationality ungar
Nationalität

Adresse Györ Opitz Ferenc u. 14

Fingerprint
Fingerabdruck

Ungarisches Komitee

Signature Csillag János
Unterschrift

Weimar-Buchenwald, am 25. Mai...

Official Buchenwald ID for liberated prisoners.

Searching for family graves - with my sons in Györ Jewish cemetery.

56

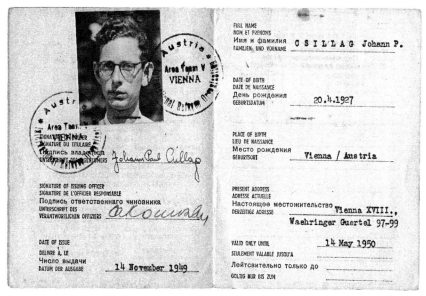

International Refugee Organisation Passport/ID, (Today's equivalent of an asylum seeker's ID).

*Ship to a new life in
Australia
The USNS General M. B.
Stewart.*

*Guthega Power Station, Snowy Mountains, NSW – where my
wife and I worked, met and married.*

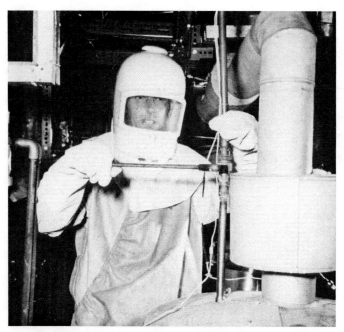

Working in the laboratories of the Australian Atomic Energy Commission.

At the European Disability Congress, ILO, Torino.

Audrey, my wife. *Myself, 2003.*

The next generations – my children and grandchildren.